1

One sunny day, our family went for a beach walk. Lincoln, Flint, and his mate, Maison, were very excited. They loved beachcombing. We planned our walk first. We wore long pants and hats to keep the sun off. We filled up our water bottles and set off.

2

3

The beach had lots of sticks and dry bull kelp. We were glad we wore our boots! Lincoln ran in and out of the water, finding things. Flint and Maison found some tumbleweed in the sand dunes. They had a great time rolling it along the beach! Boandik kids have been playing with these for many years.

Knowledge Books and Software

5

The boys saw so many different things along the way. They found drift bottles and old craypot floats. There was bull kelp and brown kelp and red, fluffy seaweed that looked like feathers. Our ancestors ate this seaweed and we still do now. They even found a leafy sea dragon that had washed up on the shore.

Knowledge Books and Software

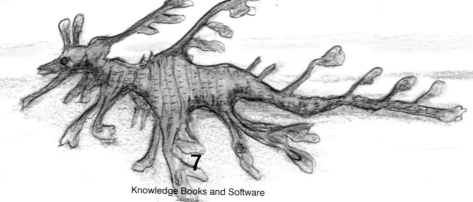

7

Bluebottles had washed up on the beach. They dried in the sun and popped as you walked on them. They even found a porcupine fish, puffed up like a football. One of their favourite finds was a cowrie shell. The cowrie shell is very special to the Boandik culture.

Knowledge Books and Software

9

We waded out to an island close to the shore. The island had a cave in the middle. It made great echoes. This cave would have been used by Boandik people many years ago. Lincoln kicked off his boots to get the sand out of them. Just then, the sea came in and washed his right boot out to sea.

Knowledge Books and Software

There was nothing we could do to save it. The water was too deep. The boys called it Robbie, the right foot boot. They went back along the beach again. Lincoln clomped the rest of the way with one boot. Mum had a picnic ready for us at the end of our walk. We headed home then, thinking that was the last we would see of Robbie.

Knowledge Books and Software

13

Robbie drifted out to sea. Along the way, dolphins played with him. They flicked him high out of the water. Turtles checked him out to see if he was a jellyfish. The squid and the octopus left him alone because he did not change colour.

Knowledge Books and Software

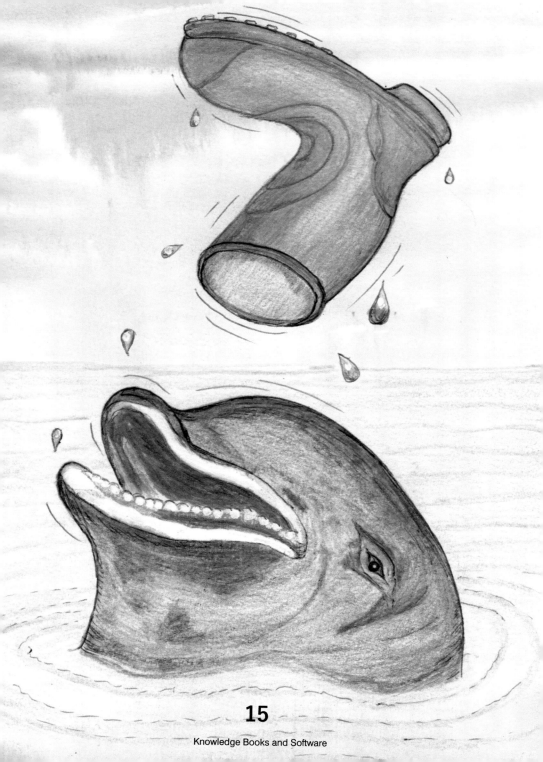

15

Some barnacles started to grow on Robbie. They gave him some shiny, blue bling! Robbie bobbed along in the current all the way down to Victoria. The sea breeze then blew him all the way back. He finally washed up at Maggoty Point (Nene Valley).

Knowledge Books and Software

17

A friend of ours called Aunty Lucie was walking along that very beach one day. Something caught her eye in the deep seaweed. It was a red, right foot rubber boot with lots of barnacles. Lucie thought this would look great hanging on the front door of her shack!

Knowledge Books and Software

19

Some weeks later, our family visited Aunty Lucie. The boys raced to the front door and knocked. While they were waiting for her, they saw the red, rubber boot. They looked at one another and then yelled out, "Mum, Dad, look! It's Robbie, on Aunty Lucie's front door!"

Knowledge Books and Software

21

Lucie opened the door and the boys told her all about their story. Everyone was surprised to see Robbie again. They talked for ages about all the adventures Robbie must have had in their sea country.

Knowledge Books and Software

Word bank

Lincoln	Boandik
Flint	island
Maison	amazing
excited	drifting
beachcombing	squid
interesting	octopus
tumbleweed	barnacles
different	Victoria
sea dragon	Maggoty
bluebottles	wonderful
porcupine	adventures
favourite	
cowrie	

Knowledge Books and Software